SEEDLINGS

The cover illustrates a dream I had shortly after discovering *The Urantia Book*. This dream demonstrates my purpose and direction, and the spiritual foundation of my life. It is further explained in the first two Seedlings.

SEEDLINGS

VOLUME ONE

∞

by Michael Hagan with Monica Kemp

Seedlings VOLUME ONe
Copyright © 2023 by Michael Hagan

Book design by River Sanctuary Graphic Arts
Cover art by Paul Kemp

All citations are from *The Urantia Book*, Chicago: Urantia Foundation, 1955.

ISBN 978-1-952194-26-9

Printed in the United States of America

Additional copies available from:

www.riversanctuarypublishing.com
amazon.com

Proceeds from sale of this book go to the *Center for Unity* through the *Worldwide Ministry of Jesus*

RIVER SANCTUARY PUBLISHING
P.O. Box 1561
Felton, California 95018
www.riversanctuarypublishing.com

Dedicated to the awakening of the New Earth

Acknowledgements

My wife Joan has seen me through countless hours for over a year while I wrote almost daily. Monica Kemp has, from the beginning supported, edited, and advised me on each story and helped me dispel doubt and impatience. She has been my North Star. Jimmer Prieto, creator of the website *communionbreathing.com*, has been a dedicated supporter, encouraging me from the start to believe in the spiritual value of this writing. He has done Spanish translations and advised me about getting them out into the Spanish speaking world. Jorge Krupa has posted every *Seedling* on her Facebook page and added beautiful graphics. Paul Kemp provided the cover art. Jose Espinosa has created digital animations of many *Seedlings*. Susan Lyon has formatted them. Many friends and colleagues in *The Urantia Book* Fellowship have consistently encouraged me and shared ideas.

Fifty years of reading *The Urantia Book* provided the basic truth underlying each story. It is the source of many of the concepts and some unfamiliar terminology. Several direct quotes from the book are cited. The first two stories in this collection will explain the stories' origin and guiding purpose.

Mostly, I acknowledge communion with my spiritual family as I wrote, especially with my angels and my blessed Adjuster, my Universal Father's indwelling spiritual presence without whom I could not have written these stories. He is my eternal life partner. His ideas, motivation, collaboration, and constant flow of positive spiritual energy and loving embrace of me have been essential in guiding each story to its completion. This collaboration is not usually a conscious process, but I always realize when I am working alone; those stories never go anywhere and are soon abandoned.

The symbol for infinity ∞ is a tribute to our Universal Father and to my Adjuster. This book is dedicated to them and to our beloved Creator Son, Jesus.

Contents

How I Met My Father

Fifty years ago, I was having a talk with a neighbor. I was in a rock band at the time, and Bob used to sit and listen to us practice. Usually we only shared mis-delivered mail or maybe a lawnmower. Somehow the conversation turned to religion.

He had just come across a big blue book that dealt with topics as varied as religion, history, astronomy, human relationships, and our Father's promise to join him in eternal life. As a scientist, he had found it to be accurate far ahead of the time in which it was published, and he reasoned that it was probably accurate about religion as well.

I was a year into my search for deeper spiritual truth. Bob was just beginning his. He took me into his house and showed me *The Urantia Book*. My memory of sitting in a chair in his house reading for three days is still fresh. I soon ordered my own, and never stopped reading.

As a child, I had a relationship with God as a member of his church family. Now, I was beginning to build a personal relationship with Father. Both experiences are the foundations of my spiritual life.

I learned that Jesus gave us his Spirit of Truth, his spiritual guide to surely lead me to him. It was this spirit that affirmed the truth I was discovering. Later, in a dream, I saw Father's promise illuminated. It was an indelible image of two rainbows side by side. One represented my mortal self, the other God's pure spirit fragment, my Thought Adjuster. They were joining at the base in a blue fusion. It was a promise that I would one day fuse with a fragment of God as a new spiritual being with eternal life in a loving universe.

Now, fifty years later, I know God as a Father. I feel his absolute love every day, yearn for it, desire to share it with others. His love is at the core of my being, powering my life goal of serving my sisters and brothers, writing stories about spiritual growth.

Mostly, Father is my friend. All he asks of me is that I extend that friendship to all his other children, my sisters and brothers, whether friends or adversaries. As members of his family, we are told to share his love, let it pass through us to make this a better world.

My Father has become my best friend.

A Gift From God

Before there was time and space, there was God. And before creating time and space universes in which we would one day dwell, like any wise and loving father he provided for his children. He created infinite numbers of spirit entities, fragments of his pure love, Thought Adjusters, which he would one day bestow upon us.

As the universes unfolded over eons, he nurtured these spirit fragments in preparation for the day they would indwell us, his as-yet unborn children. Stars, planets and life slowly took form.

When we were very young, these spirit fragments were eager to indwell us. They vied among themselves for the chance to join each new mortal, to begin an eternal quest to rejoin their Father on Paradise.

Once selected, they were each ready with an eternal plan which they had prepared for us, with one fundamental stipulation: it could only be enacted with our consent. They would live within us, love us, but guide us only when we asked for their guidance.

As we grew, we were daily confronted with decisions. At first, perhaps for a long time, we didn't ask for spiritual help making decisions. Sometimes they fit within the spirit fragment's plans and dreams for us, sometimes not. As each decision was made, adjustments were made to the plan as needed. But we remained in complete control of our lives. Beginning with our first moral decision as a child, a soul was born within. As these decisions multiplied, they fed our blossoming soul.

This soul, rarely detected, will continue to grow, one day to become the new us. Eventually we will be offered the opportunity to eternally identify with this soul and fuse with the fragment of God which has been anticipating this day all our lives.

Our new life as a spirit-destined child of God will be an eternity of loving education and service throughout the universes. And one day we will stand face to face with our loving Father who longs for this moment to embrace us.

Who wouldn't like to be gifted?

It Takes a Universe to Raise a Child

Good parents plan ahead. Our Dad started planning for us billions of years ago. He knew that we would need a village to grow up in, but the village would need to be on a planet and the planet would need a star. He wanted a lot of kids, so that would require a lot of stars, actually a universe full of them.

A universe takes a long time to build. To build the perfect one, He needed to think about what kids want. Once the planets were ready for life, he needed to guide life's evolution. Kids need animals, some that can be tamed and some that scare them enough to make them use their brains. A diversity of plants will provide food for the animals. Some foods are obvious, like fruits; some, like seeds, require humans to exercise imagination to unlock their secrets.

Kids hate to be bored and itch to explore, so plenty of interesting environments are in order. Kids seek out challenges and adventures. Give them mountains to climb, jungles to explore, and oceans to navigate.

As they mature, they will need guidance. Embed them in loving, supportive communities. Help them build relationships. Encourage them to transcend themselves. Give them the gift of God: a divine indwelling spirit with which they can bond. Before long they will look up to the stars and deeply into themselves.

In a short time, they will outgrow the planet. It has provided them with a beginning, whetted their appetites, but they're ready for new challenges. Why not plan the universe as a university? Give them new, spiritual bodies to live in. Provide them with the best teachers and schools, spread out over an increasingly vast, intricate, diversified super-universe. Train them as teachers, artists, scientists, and leaders.

Finally, send them to the center of the grand universe, to meet their Creators face to face for the first time. Then send them out to the new, emerging universes that will need teachers, artists, scientists, and leaders for a brand-new order of beings. Are you ready to join up with this eternal project? Just say yes to our Father and climb on board!

It takes children to build new universes.

Going My Way?

In my youth, hitchhikers were everywhere. Now, not so much. So, I decided it's time for a whole new generation of them. Let's call them "virtual hitchhikers." Like those of old, they can provide conversation for drivers on long journeys down lonesome roads. Well, not conversation so much as contemplation, not roads so much as life.

As drivers go about their daily lives, they are sometimes free (e.g., waiting in line somewhere) to mentally deal with issues large and small. A writer's job is to plant seedlings in their brains that just lurk there, ready to sprout unexpectedly.

Now, there are more roads than ever, many ways to get to the same place. Each journey is individualized, with convenient rest stops, quaint little inns, interesting detours, and new discoveries to be made. There are even new paths waiting to be opened, new trails to be blazed.

Often, when the road is monotonous, the mind is set free. The ideas/questions begin to roam inside. What did that statement mean? Why did he say it that way? Does he mean *me*?

"It's my pleasure to provoke you. Thank you!"

The alternative is pretty bleak. You go to work, raise a family, then you die. If that's enough, then read no further. You've achieved the bliss of ignorance. But I suspect you want more.

Seek out those hitchhikers. Engage them in contemplation. Take them as far as they need to go. Then go a mile further. Maybe they have friends in a book somewhere. Ask for their number, then call them from time-to-time to check in.

Keep an eye open for a thumb sticking out. Then tell 'em,

"Climb aboard."

Self-Defense Can Be Hazardous to Your Health

We live in fascinating times, most prominently the times of the virus. We vaccinate, isolate, mask, keep our distance, minimize contact with others, seek out a bubble of like-minded peers in hopes of avoiding microscopic organisms. If just a few get in and multiply we might find ourselves in mortal danger.

However, even the most successful coping strategies can still leave us vulnerable to an even more deadly disease, one as old as the human race. It too is invisible, but we have grown to live with it. We don't usually even recognize it, even though we are all infected and highly contagious.

It's often discreetly passed on through an argument, is revealed in a sideways glance or a thoughtless, perhaps well-intended but uninvited criticism. Included in a crude joke it can even make us laugh. It can be even less visible than that. It might be passed on in the failure to support someone in their time of need or missing an opportunity to enrich a relationship.

This disease is called **the human condition**.

Many of us have had experiences that hardened us, often for our own self-preservation. It isn't easy to risk love or even friendship when past experiences have proven disastrous. Inner vulnerability can be riskier than emptying a bank account, even for a sure thing.

The cure is the exact opposite of a viral vaccine. It might involve a softening here, a willingness to forgive there. These baby steps are a spiritual inoculation. Unlike a physical vaccine, they seek out and destroy the defenses you have so carefully devised, eliminate microbes of hatred, bigotry or self-serving. They strengthen your spirits and leave you a little more open to the love outside.

Yes, there can be genuine danger here. Bravery is demanded. You will be constantly challenged, often in small ways. Speak calmly when confronted, smile when discouraged, hope when all seems hopeless, respond to a harsh word with kindness, find spiritual meaning in life.

Father's love is all around you. Welcome it.

Simply accept it. You deserve it.

I've Never Lost a Fist Fight!

I've never won one either. Truth is, I've never been in one.

My specialty has been verbal bouts. I find myself all too ready to respond to a disagreement with a punch-back. I'm often tactful, sensitive, not full of myself. Okay, not often enough. But the main problem with any argument is, someone wins, and someone loses. When ego is on the line, it's not easy being a loser.

Why do I *do* that, feel the need to respond when something is said that is contrary to my belief system. Is it because of my own doubts about my hard-held position?

Arguing is counter-productive, encourages counterattacks, further entrenches an opponent in her/his point of view. The real goal should be the arrival at truth, period.

Some of my arguments have been with provocateurs, people who love to incite just for the sake of arguing. I find myself enjoying these bouts, especially if there's an audience. Lost in the moment, I abandon fellowship for points.

My hardest opponents frustrate me by not arguing back. This leaves me silent, internally stewing over my inability to land a counterpunch on an opponent who refuses to fight.

When I was a teenager, I would relentlessly argue with my mother. I'm now embarrassed by my inability to give in time and again. I remember once arguing with my teenage daughter. She told me the next day that she had realized in the middle of the argument that she was wrong but would not admit it. So *that's* what my mother put up with!

A loving response turns away wrath. We are all either growing toward or away from our Father. My priority needs to be growing closer to all, enticing others to act on spiritual values, avoiding argument and stimulating a search for truth. Kindness and truth should be the priority when discussing (not arguing) something with a friend or an opponent.

Wait, did I just say *opponent?* A brother or sister is not an enemy, and *all* are my brothers and sisters, even the ones who may have gone astray. And who am I to decide who's gone astray?

From now on I intend to avoid every verbal bout with a well thought out **TKO!**

True Kindness Opportunity.

Stormy Weather

Anger is a spirit poison. It has lurked in my subconscious all my life, waiting to be called up when provoked. As a teacher, it was always under control, never rose to interfere in my relationship with a child or a colleague. At other times, though, it was ready to spring into action.

Sadly, anger made appearances within my family. Once I unloaded it on my young daughter. She burst into tears, crying "I've just lost my daddy!" That was my low point, an abrupt wake-up call. Something needed to be done.

An earlier experience dealing with the topic of anger occurred when I was 19. It came as the culmination of a systematic re-examination of my religious beliefs, my church upbringing. One by one I peeled away doctrines I no longer believed in, the virgin birth, atonement for our sins, and, deepest of all, Jesus' perfection. I concluded, after thinking about Jesus' righteous indignation and forceful "clearing of the temple," that he had displayed anger and was therefore not perfect after all. I now know better.

I slowly began rebuilding a spiritual life, exploring eastern religions and other teachings, culminating in the discovery of Jesus' life and teachings and God's absolute love for us, his children.

Anger has not cropped up for a long time now. The stormy weather of my youth is subsiding into memory. Like a dormant volcano, though, it rumbles now and then, threatening to spill over. I'm learning to develop true self-respect, and to treat my brothers and sisters with the respect they deserve. Anger and hate will destroy us. Only love can save us from ourselves.

There's LOVE in the forecast!

This Just Isn't Fair

Our daughters, like all children, were sticklers for fairness. We finally heard of a good way to deal with that, at least for the *"candy bar problem."* You know the one: "Her half is bigger than mine. This isn't fair!" The solution we found was simple; one daughter cuts the candy in half, the other gets first choice of which half is hers. You could've weighed those halves to the gram. The fights stopped, at least *those* fights.

For adults, though, there is no simple solution, especially with the way we perceive fairness in our lives; the way we feel Father treats us. The biggest complaint, heard most often "Why is there so much inequality and suffering in the world? If God loves us, how could he let *this happen?*"

Two reasons stand out. Our planet isn't finished yet, and neither are we. Let's begin with the planet, specifically when natural disasters destroy homes through so-called Acts of God. **WHAT!** *Global warming is God's fault?*

We understand enough about planetary evolution to agree that, compared to its fiery beginning, Earth is pretty livable. Sure, there are natural disasters, but wise planning on our part can mitigate the dangers. For example, avoid building homes on proven fault zones and near volcanos. Homes built in tornado country need to be stronger, with built-in shelters. Am I missing something here?

But there are also plenty of man-made building disasters which can be mitigated by creating and following safe building codes, and simply caring enough about our sisters and brothers to plan with everyone's needs and safety in mind, not just those of the elite. In fact, human activity and values are at the very core of every situation. Greed, selfishness, racism, poor planning, and global warming are problems humans created, not God.

Human problems. Like the planet, *we aren't finished yet*. Maybe it's time to stop blaming Father and agree that we need to find an honest way to split the candy bar. Wise parents don't give their children everything they want, solve their problems for them or make life too easy. They expect their children to take care of themselves, solve their own problems, love and value each other.

Did I say there was no simple way? There is. It's called choosing God's will instead of our own. That's easily said, but it requires dedicated thinking, a willingness to reflect before acting, a need to widen human bandwidth, to sacrifice personal wealth, to pray and worship.

Father gave us a pretty good deal. He created a beautiful planet, stocked it with amazing plants and animals, helped us evolve, sent loving spiritual guides to live among and within us, and offered to help us solve problems by working with him, choosing his will above our own. And now,

Maybe it's just time to *STOP WHINING!*

Who's in Charge Around Here?

Forty-five years ago, I stood in my kitchen, showing my dad the remodeling work I had just completed. His comment was, "Good job, Mike." That was high praise coming from him. He and my grandfather were master carpenter/cabinet makers and didn't give compliments lightly. That was all the encouragement I needed. I've since remodeled two more houses, each time setting my goals higher than the time before.

As hard as carpentry is to master, it's child's play compared to the challenges of self-mastery. Jesus, a master carpenter and boatbuilder, once said, "He who masters himself is greater than he who conquers a city." For the longest time, I didn't understand what that really meant. I equated self-mastery with diets or abandoning bad habits. It's a cosmic question. Self, or God; *who is your master*? You cannot serve both.

Jesus had learned from childhood that the path of spiritual embrace with God far transcends the path of self. The challenge of our lives is to become like a child, humbly listen to Father, devote our lives to him and to our sisters and brothers.

I once asked myself, when tempted to engage in a life-long bad habit, a personal pet evil, if I would do that in front of my earthly father. Then I reflected on my divine Father and angels having to witness it. The more I began to realize the spiritual world was real, the more that habit began to lose its allure.

Evils give us pleasure, and body and mind don't like to give up pleasurable pursuits. As St. Augustine once said, "God, make me chaste and celibate...but not just yet." I've given up many bad habits. But self-improvement, will power, is only part of self-mastery. True self-respect is the final goal. It isn't about looking into the mirror but looking into the soul.

The "incessant clamoring of an inescapable self" is slowly receding as I master myself, choose Father over self. My quest for a living spiritual connection with him is unfolding. I will soon travel the universes for eternity, always getting closer to him, only to discover that he is more loving than I ever dreamed.

I can't wait to hear my Heavenly Father say,

"Good Job, Mike!"

My New Friend

Suppose one day you made the acquaintance of someone you had long known of and admired but never really met, someone you knew traveled in higher circles than you. You had long assumed that you would not be able to relate with someone that far above you. Surprisingly you got along well, and on more and more occasions got together.

Eventually you became friends. You discovered you could trust each other and confide at deep levels. A kinship was developing, a mutual affection. Your relationship was growing, deepening.

One day your new friend invited you to travel together on an extended journey, to which you readily agreed. Together you visited amazing, far away, and beautiful places, met new and intriguing people, and took on incredible tasks. You were gaining new skills and insights, all the while humbled by your new friend's astonishing abilities.

Your new friend increasingly shared a magnificent past with you as well, going back long before you had met. All these experiences, past and present, began to become a real, richer part of your own life.

Your friendship steadily deepened into a lasting bond of love and commitment. Gradually you became inseparable, often finishing each other's sentences. You two were now one.

An inconceivable possibility? Not really. It is available to all, high and low, young, and old, rich and poor, righteous and unrighteous. This friend exists within each of us, guiding and supporting us every minute of every day, yearning for our friendship and eventual eternal bonding. This inner spirit is of God, is pure love. And all we are asked to do is say "Yes," then proceed on that journey.

This will be the beginning of a great friendship.

After-Life Insurance

I just got off the phone with an insurance claims adjuster. My truck had been stolen, now recovered, but several personal items – a house key, a key for another car, and a wedding ring were gone. I learned for the first time that, though my auto policy was up to date, those things would not be covered. They were not "factory installed." If you turn the car upside down, anything that falls out would not be covered by this policy.

It later occurred to me that I also have life insurance, but with a different company. That policy is also up to date, and it is ironclad: no deductible, no exclusions, no need to spend time on the phone with an agent. In fact, I acquired it for free! It is my Get Out of Jail Free card... that is, Get Off the Earth Free. I have signed a contract with a company named...? Let's call it, Celestial Life and Casualty.

Wait..., did I say no exclusions? Actually, when this life is over, "turned upside down," things that "fall out of my pocket" – money, house, car, investments, possessions, are not covered. All material things are gone, including my "factory-made" body. But my soul will carry on.

A clause in my contract stipulates that I will get a fresh start with a new body and live on a beautiful mansion world. I will meet for the first time my new life partner, a fragment of God's pure love. I will mingle with others who came from similar yet unique backgrounds, be educated in the finest schools, be given a series of amazing new jobs, receive regular promotions, and ultimately get an all-expenses paid trip around the universe.

Wait... did I say free? Yes, at first it *is* free, no questions asked, no baggage too heavy. Just say yes. But there are installments to be made: new habits to acquire, positive attitudes to master, regular meetings with our Father to learn how to grow up to be just like Him.

That knock on your door...? It's opportunity.

Your Adjuster awaits your signature.

There's Something Fishy Going On Around Here

I was raised in a little town in Oregon, with forest as a back yard and meadows and streams as playgrounds. I would go swimming and fishing in idyllic parts of the Umpqua River, enjoy fresh-caught trout at family picnics.

Now in Silicon Valley, I no longer do any fishing, at least not for fish. I now fish for stories, and souls. Sometimes I get a nibble as I'm driving or worshiping. But my favorite fishing hole is in my head, as I awaken in the early morning. I commune with Father, asking him if he has any good ideas to share. He passed along this one today.

These fish, the stories I share, don't suffer from hooks. They eagerly splash around, almost luring *me* instead of the other way around. If I'm hooked, I make a note so as not to forget them, then dedicate the beginning of the day to putting their natural beauty on paper.

Father works alongside me to get the story just right. He is not only a master fisherman, but also a master storyteller. Before our collaboration began, I was an enthusiastic but mediocre writer. Now our lines that flow onto paper are seamless and bright.

Unlike the fish I once caught, these stories are "catch-and-release." They are crafted as best as I can do, shared with my partner Monica for final editing, inspection, and approval. Ready for release, they then become "free-range" stories, launched into cyberspace.

Since they are not owned by anyone, they are fair game for the next fisherwoman/fisherman who catches them. In new hands and minds, they can be shared with others or become hybridized, acquire a new accent or new idioms more appropriate for a different language or culture.

They are free to roam the world, seeking spiritual minds in which to grow, then emerge anew. Hopefully, they will become transformed as they travel, changing lives and minds. I know they've changed *mine* as they've passed through; writers learn from their own writing.

Jesus challenged his apostles, and all of us, to become fishers of men. We are told not to rest until his gospel of love, the Fatherhood of God and brotherhood of man, has conquered and transformed the world. I have in turn dedicated my life to helping make that happen. And I have been blessed with partners, sisters and brothers who are also dedicated fishing enthusiasts.

Let's all become Fisherwomen/Men!

Devoted to You

In every life there are profound events, indelibly etched into our awareness, fundamentally altering us. My most powerful was an experience of overwhelming spiritual embrace, Father's love for me. Before then I'd been cognitively aware of it; suddenly I was aware of his love at every level simultaneously. I also remember the first time later when I felt and sent the same wave of love to *him*. It was a spiritual rebirth, like experiencing a volcanic eruption. Shock and awe.

A volcanic event is often followed by a steady flow of lava, rebuilding the earth, gradually forming the foundation for new growth. My relationship with Father follows the same pattern, is being rebuilt on an ever more solid basis. The lava of each event continues to flow steadily, undramatically, daily affirming.

New love can be dazzling, overwhelming. As it transitions into daily, enduring love, it gives off steady warmth at a deep level. Lovingly nurtured, it becomes devotion, profound dedication.

Lava, love, driven deeper inside by rain and storms, is transformed into rich loam supportive of new life. The earth, my life, welcomes the richness of this soil, yields the fruits of the spirit.

Daily worship has now become part of my life. Before, I was skeptical of worship, saw it as foreign to me, unnatural. I stuck with it, gently nudging my consciousness when it strayed, patiently putting in the time. Then one day I felt a sensation of outreach, as though there was a lifeline reaching out from me. A living spiritual connection was growing. That image endures with me, compels me.

When I was first taught how to worship, I was told to find a word that I could bring up when I felt myself mentally wandering. I chose love, then Father. I was told the word didn't matter. Now that word has been changed once again, to profound dedication...

Devotion

Will This Be on the Final?

I retired fifteen years ago from teaching and had a retirement celebration. I will again retire in another fifteen years, from Earth. Unfortunately, there won't be a final retirement party here. Since mourning is the custom, it'll be a more somber event. Too bad because it's a really great opportunity for a big party.

Instead of a joyful retirement party, I'll have a joyful welcoming party on a mansion world attended by post-mortal and spiritual friends. But before the party comes the Final Exam. The achievements and failures of my life will be laid bare for evaluation. It will reveal both victories to celebrate and defeats to learn from.

Final exams are usually fear-ridden, anxious events. Did I really learn the lesson? Will I earn a passing grade or fail? No cheating allowed; my celestial friends, my Adjuster and the angels, know me better than I know myself.

I'm not worried, though. I've already been assured that I will pass the test. We all can. In fact, it's a guaranteed pass, even if you've done *only one thing right in your whole life!* What is that? Say "Yes" to the universe by desiring to team up with Dad to love God and serve your fellows.

He offers us the most precious gift possible, fusion with a fragment of him. This union will become a newly minted being with amazing spiritual potential. It's that easy. I feel his love as I write.

Oh yeah, there's one catch (always read the fine print). High expectations come with this offer. Even though you will be joyfully accepted into a new spiritual reality, it won't be a life of ease. You won't be sitting on a cloud eating bonbons for eternity.

The work begins day one and will never be finished. But remember, Jesus said, "My burden is light, and my yoke is easy." Here on earth and throughout vast universes there are those in need of your love and commitment, and you will have lots of spiritual help.

Where do you apply? What job do you want? I found it was as easy as asking my guardian angel persistently for an assignment. Eventually, a job opened. It was custom-made for me, not easy but highly rewarding, with new, blessed friends as co-workers and plenty of spiritual support.

You'll Ace this final exam!

I'm NOT a Baby!!!

Close your eyes, shut the door, you don't have to worry anymore,
I'll be your baby tonight.

My wife Joan and I have a classic routine: she lovingly refers to me as "Baby," to which I adamantly, whiningly, respond, "I'm **NOT** a baby!" Her next line is "You're my baby." Her next line is sung, "I'll be your baby tonight."

Tears. Our deepest love brings with it tears.

A few days ago, as I was going about my bread-making routines, I was suddenly struck with my love for Jesus. I had to grab hold of the counter, began sobbing uncontrollably, saying "I love you, Jesus." I made no attempt to regain my composure, but eventually I did. Never have I enjoyed such a profound wave of love for our Brother/ Father. I thank him for it repeatedly. Humans need to be known in order to be loved. Father needs to be loved in order to be known.

Men don't cry! Be a man! Snap out of it! We men have long been taught by our culture to eschew emotions, be stoic, *man up*! All along, women have known much better, have shed tears of sorrow and joy, have embraced emotions as the cleansing touchstones of a deeper life.

When a friend taught worship techniques to a group of us, he suggested a way to redirect our wandering, human minds back to worship, as they so often need be gently steered. "Choose a word, any word, to help you gently re-focus toward father." I had several words that I used, but recently settled on the word *devotion*. My love for Father is personal, even romantic.

Today, as I worshipped, that romantic love for him began to overwhelm me, so much so that I could not remain in worship. It's as though I was responding to a news bulletin on TV... "We interrupt this worship for an important announcement. You are advised to seek the nearest computer immediately and begin this story. This is not a test."

I have felt his overwhelming wave of love take over my whole body a few times, every ultimaton inside me vibrating. We are all blessed to have a relationship with him, and he yearns to give us his love; unfortunately, we lack the wavelength to continuously receive what he unceasingly sends. No, I don't cultivate spiritual tears, but I do embrace them.

I Am My Father's Son.

Climbing Out of the Wreckage

In September of 1988, from a hospital bed, I began to emerge from a coma and rebuild my life. I discovered that a week earlier I had suffered a major stroke. I couldn't walk, talk, write or feed myself. I could barely move. My consciousness was trapped in my own body, unable to be expressed. My wife was told not to expect me to survive. My body, my life vehicle, had been nearly totaled. In a sense, I needed to be reborn.

Jesus taught that we must enter God's family as a child, with the primal trust a child has in its caregivers. Now, like a child, I was vulnerable. I had to learn anew to trust caregivers for basic needs. It was not an easy lesson, and I was a real brat!

Like a survivor of a car crash, I slowly climbed from the wreckage. I began rehabilitation, spent years (and continue to be) re-learning how to walk, to talk, to write, to play guitar, to eat without choking.

Child-like trust is priceless, almost a once-in-a-lifetime gift. It is our first, most important lesson in life, all too easily forgotten, sometimes even crushed. We yearn to be as competent and as wise as the adults we see around us. We trust in and emulate them, later transferring that trust to Father. It is the first, most important step in our life-long journey to achieve union with Him.

Humbling yourself is not "natural" in our culture. We're constantly bombarded with "be manly/womanly" reminders: "Stand up for yourself!" "Don't give in!" "You're number one!" "It's all about you!" "Win at all costs!" "Put away childish things."

Reborn children of God are child-*like*, not child-*ish*. They don't wear the armor of pride, the veneer of invulnerability. They aren't jaded know-it-alls. They are willing and eager to learn, to share, to love, to be of good cheer.

It's never too late to re-learn to love Father. He will not disappoint you, will lift you up to the stature of true mutual and self-respect. Each day, reconnect with the simple joy of being his child,

learn to trust Daddy.

I'm a Dumpster Diver,
and Proud of It!

For many years I was allowed by a local hardwoods retailer to do daily dumpster dives, after I realized the wealth of discarded lumber trimmings in the dumpster out back. Scraps of oak, maple, walnut, Honduras mahogany, cherry, sometimes highly figured, exquisite wood, were there for the picking.

In my home wood shop those trimmings were glued, clamped and planed, then crafted into bookshelves, a stereo cabinet, a complete kitchen remodel, and many other projects. There remains a vast supply of wood, more than I have time to use.

For millions of people around the world, often children, this is not a hobby but instead a survival strategy. And, like me, they should be proud of their many hours spent recycling or refashioning the sometimes-valuable discards tossed aside in our disposable world.

Our Father is the best dumpster diver in the universe! He is constantly poring through the human rejects of our world. He sees potential where others see only trash. He works non-stop, restoring discarded souls.

Whenever possible, he doesn't do this alone. He seeks out or trains master crafts-persons, sends them out as needed to get to work restoring his precious children. He doesn't rest as long as there is a chance to give peace, love, and happiness to every member his family.

That homeless person you just stumbled upon, that former convict who seeks a new start, that obnoxious member of your work staff... each of them deserves a loving and dedicated dumpster diver. Be ready to join in on the universe's *reduce/reuse/recycle* campaign. Seek out the highest honor in God's universe, the opportunity and privilege of discovering and doing his will by helping one of his children.

Dive deep

How I Met My Guardian Angel

Yes, that's right, I was going along, doing my spiritual study, deepening my relationship with Father, when I met my guardian angel. Theresa, a South African friend, introduced us, so I named my angel Teresa. One day, we'll be formally introduced. I'll meet her and her partner face-to-face and learn their real names. I expect a full spiritual embrace after all we've done together.

Theresa and I were in a Zoom meeting. She happened to mention that she had discovered a YouTube site of a choir singing a hymn, "Guardian Angel from Heaven so bright." I found it, listened, and experienced the vibrant, loving embrace of my own guardian angel. The same thing happens every time I have listened to it since. I now speak to, and thank her, every day.

I have learned how deeply our guardian angels love us, are charged with caring for us during our lives here on earth, eager to one day join us in eternal life traveling the universes. I know the love mine has for me. What awaits me is an even more profound love than I am currently capable of perceiving.

My spiritual quest has been a long one. I am learning more daily about the unseen spiritual reality in which we are immersed, what it offers to and expects of us. I discovered the importance of asking Teresa to open doors of service for me. My worship of Father needs to be balanced with service of my fellows.

Months of persistently asking for an assignment finally paid off. My first, my current assignment, was to write stories. Father, Mother and Teresa know what I can do and like to do, made arrangements for that job to open up, then gave me a nudge in the right direction and a lot of help ever since. A second job just opened up, assisting inmates seeking spiritual guidance. These aren't easy jobs, but I'm learning how to do them. They are a joy, a blessing, and a privilege.

It may sound a little odd, to ask that my life be made *more difficult.* I've retired after thirty-three years of teaching. I deserve a long break. Maybe, after these assignments are completed... unless...

Please Sir, may I have some more?

A Leap of Faith

Ever stood on a high-dive board far above the water, gathering up the courage to jump into space for the first time? How about a cliff overlooking a lagoon? Or an outcropping of rock into the ocean?

Imagine being an olympic athlete, on the precipice of a ski jump, ready to travel at astonishing speed, then begin a series of twists and turns while plummeting back to earth. How strong is your faith in all the coaching, practice and preparation of a lifetime? Are you ready to draw on that faith, put your life on the line? Few of us would dare to put themselves at a level of risk that high.

A life well-lived is full of even greater risks: choosing the right life partner, making a timely career move, or raising children in an uncertain world. We don't always have the full information or insight needed to make the choice. But it must be made. And choices are often encountered when we feel least prepared, must be made immediately, might never be available again. <u>Choices are crucial to growth</u>.

And the ultimate choice is before us all day, every day. At any given moment we are confronted with the choice between our Father's will and our own. The decision is usually much less profound than whether or not to jump from a high cliff. It might be as simple as deciding how to respond to an unkind remark or taking the time to help someone in need.

Like the olympic ski jumper, a lifetime of training and small decisions pave the way for making big decisions about how to act: *character*.

How well have we listened to our own inner coach, the spirit fragment of our Father, preparing us to navigate life's large and small ski jumps? How instinctively do we put the needs of others above our own? What would Jesus do? How much faith do we really have in his promise of eternal life? Do we have enough faith in that promise to choose, every time, to do our Father's will?

A leap is made easier when you listen to your inner spiritual coach/ friend counseling you, calling out a dare to encourage you to trust him and yourself. Because *faith is a dare*. Do I *dare* to have faith in Father? What worldly treasure am I willing to give up for his sake? Do I really believe in a universe full of loving spiritual guides, all part of a loving family ready and eager to help me? Will God have my back?

Go ahead, have faith. I dare you!

A Friend in Need is a Friend in Deed

There are many kinds of friends. Casual acquaintances are the most common, a comfortable community for work, school, or socializing. Transactional friends are there for us, and we for them, but only for specific needs. Needy friends rely on us for emotional, financial, or social support; we care for them but their ability to reciprocate is limited. And there are fair-weather friends... enough said about them.

True friends are much more precious and rarer. Few limits are imposed upon their mutual support, freely shared. True friends are those for whom we are willing to make the greatest, even the ultimate sacrifice. My Beloved Father Fragment/Best Friend Forever within is just such a friend. He is the only friend throughout my life on earth who has never failed me, always listened to me, always been there when I needed him, guided me through some treacherous experiences.

Our conversations have been a little one-sided. (If only I'd bought those Spiritual Hearing Aids available from Celestial Supplies). Although he talks to my soul all the time, I'm still learning how to listen. Now and then, a wonderful idea occurs to me. Him? Best not speculate. I've shared with him a lot and know that he understands me even better than I understand myself. He made me what I am today, a truth seeker.

We've been friends for almost 70 years. During that time, he has helped me through some tight spots. He has always been my unfailing support, loves me just as I am, without preconditions. He is, above all else, my truest friend. He wants to team up with me for eternity. We've promised to each other to do so, and our word is our bond.

One day we'll meet face to face. After a loving embrace, we'll have a lot to catch up on. I know he will have some great stories to share with me, with new insights into our earth-life experiences. We'll laugh heartily, long into the night, on that first day.

He will soon begin to share with me his plans for our future. Together, we will tackle some difficult tasks, love, and serve Father, attend some insightful classes, meet millions of fellow truth-seekers, travel throughout vast universes, then meet up in Paradise with our Universal Father, Eternal Son, and Infinite spirit. After that, there will be no limits to the potential for our friendship.

Do you need a true friend? Just open your heart and soul.

There's one there, waiting.

My Favorite Career

What pet is more loyal and loving than a dog? I'll never forget our first family dog. My brothers and I couldn't have had a better friend. I remember one occasion when it fought off a dog that threatened us. And playful? Just invite a dog to play and it will go into play mode, feet outstretched, head down, ready to spring into action. Let the games begin!

Last night, in a spiritual study group, someone made a comment about our even *more* loyal, loving friends, the angels. Someone had mentioned a reluctance to ask too much of our spiritual friends. He smiled as he imitated a dog ready and eager to play, bouncing up joyfully. "The angels are just as eager as them to help *us*. They *beg* us to ask them for help!"

Have you ever loved helping a child, enjoyed their glee when a game is begun, a problem solved, or a question answered? As a teacher, I remember vividly the day I was working with a first grader who had been struggling with reading. She held a book as she suddenly connected the print with the story, she knew it contained, read it fluently, then exclaimed proudly, "I can read!!!" Every time I see her now, I remind her of that moment, which she still remembers, years later, as vividly as I do.

My wife, also a lifelong teacher, spends her days volunteering with a former teaching partner because she loves children so much. She occasionally works as a substitute (they're in short supply these days; besides, doing so became her ticket to be able to volunteer during the COVID days), but prefers to volunteer for free. I share her thrill when helping a single child without the need to focus on a whole group of kids, working with one as if they are the only student in the world.

Angels are our close cousins in this world, only a little more advanced in spirituality than we are. Like a loving teacher or parent, they take delight in helping us. In fact, I'm sure that when angels get a break from serving us as an assignment (everyone deserves a break), they volunteer for more service as a restful, joyous activity.

One day, I "met" my guardian angel as I listened to a choir sing about them. Teresa (my name for her) embraced me lovingly, filling my body with an overwhelming spiritual glow. I'd been praying to her for weeks, asking her to give me a way to serve, give me a job. And she did.

I'm doing that job right now.

Beware! I Am Contagious!

I confess. I may be a super-spreader. Come in contact at your own risk.

Recently, I have been conspiring with an Accomplice to spread a new virus into the world. Actually, it is a new variant of an ancient virus. Those who catch it will experience the following symptoms:

A growing sense of humility, not self-abasement but an unusual tendency to see oneself as a small part of something larger than life.

An emerging suspicion that accumulating possessions is not the most important thing in life.

A loss of interest in being seen as the most important person in their immediate surroundings.

A tendency to talk to unseen Beings.

Becoming generous in all ways, both materially and in relationships.

For most, this virus will last only a few days, a brief interruption followed by resumption of a comfortable, self-centered life. For some it will suggest long term change, perhaps even "intensive care," as they think deeply about their lives and ponder new spiritual directions. A few will become long-haulers, their lives transformed by this virus.

The luckiest, the hardiest, will themselves become super-spreaders. They will not rest until they have done everything possible to spread this *benign virus of love* to the corners of their experience, maybe the corners of the earth.

Take note. There is no known vaccine, no pill designed to foster any level of immunity. At some time in your life, if not already, you will encounter it. When you do, look deeply inside. Allow God's spirit that lives within you to guide your reaction.

But avoid recovery at all costs!

Tears of Joy

We enter this vale of tears in tears, naked and powerless. Given a life not quite understood, we slowly learn the skills required to navigate our world of nativity. Some make an understandable choice to live this life, then, exiting, leave it behind and simply return to the dust from which they came.

But the Father's hope for our experience is that we engage in the perils of life on such a planet, slowly accumulate life skills required to protect ourselves as infants and grow closer to him. During that struggle we must make daily decisions: do we serve our own will or the will of God who provided us with the very chance to do so?

We were born into this world, struggling to survive, for the very purpose of the struggle itself. We were meant to suffer these hardships; they are our birthright. A chick cannot survive if deprived of the effort to escape a protective, then confining eggshell, its first home. So too must we struggle to make sense of this world, survive, then transcend it. Our soul, our destiny is crafted, nurtured, in the womb of travail. Daily we are called upon to forge new growth even while immersed in the fiery crucible of life.

Later we're challenged to strip away, refine this life, create a spirit-based soul. The ultimate purpose served by rebuilding ourselves as spiritual beings who have triumphed over tribulation is to re-embrace the vulnerable state into which we were first born. It is that state, once again tender and open to life, to which we are meant to return.

Only the trust of a child will carry us into our new reality, a spiritual life. Having built that new and better self, we must then prepare to shed the earthly shell which has carried us to this day.

From the dust we were born, to the dust we return. A seedling is planted into the earth to bring a new being into the stars. Father, Mother, the angels, and we have nourished our embryonic soul so deep in the womb of life. Discarding our shell as we exit this life, we finish the process of leaving the earth which has carried us to the spirit's edge. We must then shed this earthly home to reach our final place among the stars. The universe awaits us with joyful, loving, open arms.

Behold, Universe, Here Comes a Brand-New Bundle of Joy!

Pets

I've had 'em all; dogs, cats (eight litters of kittens), birds, lizards, snakes, rats, mice, turtles, frogs and butterflies (raised from eggs, then released). For 20 years my boa constrictor, Spot, was a classroom pet. Maybe I was channeling Noah. But not one of these critters begins to compare with Lizzy's influence on my life.

More than once Lizzy saved my life and defended me from assault. He got me out of jams that didn't appear survivable. He used his wiles to keep me from dangers large and small. For years, Lizzy was my truest friend.

The truth is, most of those predicaments were caused by Lizzy in the first place. He could be unruly, profane, self-serving, even evil at times. Again and again, I had to cage him, get needed help to get him back under control. But he loved me, I'll give him that.

Yes, unlike most pets, Lizzy isn't always tame. And expensive? Lizzy has cost me dearly over and over. Unruly? He has upended my life more times than I care to recite. However, to this day we are inseparable. Oddly, at times I suspect I have been Lizzy's pet all along. It's been 74 years since we first met, and his influence, though in decline, is always there.

As you may have guessed, Lizzy is my lizard brain, my ego. And he will be with me till the end of this life. He is slowly being replaced by my soul-mind, which is gradually taking over spiritual control.

The sleepless nights and anxiety he once provoked so well can now be assuaged by our Father when I ask for help.

Farewell, Lizzy.
Return to the dust from which you came.

I Don't Believe

Our young daughters firmly believed in Santa Claus. We played along, even leaving cookies on the hearth. We later eased Santa's transition into mythical status. Christmas is still a time of believing in things greater than us. Children may believe in Santa, but they'll never meet him, never really know him. Beliefs are important, but they're only the surface. They need to be explored and deepened.

As my own spiritual life grew, I believed in God but did not really *know Him*. I had a highly developed belief base that motivated me in powerful ways as I raised a family and enjoyed a career in early childhood education. That solid base, my belief system, was like a sure path to God through a vast forest.

I knew I could find him; had faith he would be found. I had a reliable map, an amazing Guide, fellow searchers who loved and guided each other, and some solid clues. But the search, through the forest called daily life, was impeded by thickets of distractions, false leads, sometimes pure fatigue.

One day I suddenly came across an opening in the canopy. The Son shone through. His warmth and light were overpowering. For a few moments I absorbed the glow. Even after it faded, I knew I was on the right path, felt a new sense of his love for me. Those moments of clarity are too few and fleeting, but they are indelible. They lend new depth and purpose to everyday life.

We live in a world with limited spiritual vision, which provides inconsistently trustworthy spiritual leadership. Our path is not always clearly illuminated. We struggle each day to clear the weeds, stay on solid footing, find the opening in the forest, finally bask in its spiritual glow. And we must find it for ourselves.

I once sat in a theater watching a documentary on Carl Jung. An early associate of Freud, Jung later transitioned from a purely scientific to a more spiritual base for psychiatry. In the interview, he was asked if he believed in God. Jung paused, then began... "Do I believe? No..." (Titters of "I knew it!" rippled through the audience.) Then he concluded with, "I don't believe...

I know!

Can You Hear Me, Now?

No, I didn't know Alexander Graham Bell personally, I'm not *that* old. But I still remember REgent 65774, our phone number when I was twelve.

RE (73) was a prefix when I was a teenager, no area code required. And I remember the first portable phones- portable if you had a wheelbarrow. Now we can carry a phone in our pocket.

But have you heard of the newest innovation? *The ME Phone!* It's a simple software download. This phone needs no charger or cable; it's recharged internally. Utilizing your body chemistry and electrical signals, it can be recharged without messy cables. Unfortunately, that makes it vulnerable. Some things consumed can cause interference. It must be housed in a body of clean habits to perform optimally. Extremely serious abuse risks loss of connection.

Reception is variable; some people will experience clarity, while others will get spotty, garbled reception, or no obvious results at all. Personal bandwidth plays a significant role in performance. There are steps that must be taken over time to overcome these liabilities, involving daily periods of silence and fine-tuning to the Central Processing Unit.

Except in the case of concussion or brain injury, it is immune to cracked screens or other serious damage. This download can obviously, unlike a physical phone, never be shared with a friend. However, you are encouraged to show others how to use their own!

It comes with an amazing plan. *It's absolutely free!* There's a lifetime warranty and no monthly user fees. Its manufacturer, Celestial Cell, promises service in any location, claiming it will even reach the center of the universe. (When used as directed; consult your Blue Pages directory for details.) Receive free upgrades, and never suffer dropped calls!

I'm not just a salesman, I'm also a customer! I've had one all my life, although I spent many years not really knowing how to use it. In fact, most of us received this download during childhood. Act now and become eligible for an eternal universe voyage! Act later, and you will simply regret the lost time.

This unlimited offer comes with an optional lifetime contract.

Buried Treasure

Buried treasure fascinates us, whether as a dream of vast riches or a window into understanding ancient times. We've all read stories of people happening upon priceless relics, gold coins, dinosaur fossils, missing links, or answers to mysteries long shrouded in obscurity.

What price would you pay to discover any of these? How willing are you to risk everything on the chance of becoming wealthy, rolling around like Scrooge McDuck in a vast pool of wealth?

However, as we well know, money won't buy happiness. The annals of overnight success are littered with stories of people who have reaped tragedy in the wake of sudden, unearned fortune.

Jesus once spoke a parable of someone discovering a treasure in a field, then immediately giving all that he had to acquire that property. But the real treasures, Jesus taught us, were spiritual. Unlike material wealth, spiritual treasure fills the soul to overflowing. But these treasures cannot be hoarded in a swimming pool. They can only belong to us when given away.

Buried treasure might be discovered suddenly, while spiritual treasures are uncovered a bit at a time. Rather than overwhelm, they might provoke no more than the lifting of an eyebrow. Whenever we abstain from criticism, respond to anger with a soft voice, lend a hand, or encourage someone, we accumulate it. Unlike material wealth, it is not visible, provable, apparent. And spiritual treasures cannot be stolen.

Unlike a chance encounter with free hidden riches, earning spiritual treasure will come at a steep price. It might mean backing down from a confrontation or humbling yourself. How willing are you to risk material wealth for spiritual gain? Or to hold your tongue when wronged, acknowledge a mistake, or seek forgiveness? The decision about where to dig is easier than the decision about where to give.

Happy hunting!

A Bountiful Harvest

One night a seed was gently planted in my brain, an idea for a story. Not an unusual experience, but an idea worth considering. I imagined the story's shape, its nuances, its purpose. It was still there the next day, germinating. I decided to give it a try.

That day, as I wrote, the story flowed with an ease I don't often feel. Like any birth it was an effort, but at the same time effortless and rewarding. It was finished that day. The same thing occurred a few days later, then again, the next.

By this time, I recognized a pattern. A writer all my life, this was not how I normally worked. I was sensing guidance. I now realize that I was entering into a spiritual partnership with my Adjuster and angels. Many of the stories so far have been in fact autobiographical, exploring that partnership and its purpose. I don't work alone.

The stories are planted as seeds in my mind, not verbally, just "thoughts" that prompt me. They may be encouraged by a line from a song, a piece of a conversation, a news event, an interaction, a worship experience, a catch phrase, gardening, running errands, a casual observation, or just a word. Simply living my life. But there is always a spark, a feeling that there's more to this casual idea than meets the eye. At those times, I rush to the computer and get to work. I've rarely been disappointed in that chain of events. Once planted in my head, the seed grows into a seedling. Sometimes I sit and try to think of these stories all on my own. Those are usually dead ends.

As the stories accumulated, I felt the need to share them. I put one out to a few people and got a response from Monica. We quickly realized we were kindred spirits. We shared strategies, passed stories back and forth, honing each one until we were satisfied before moving on to the next. This went on for months. Finally, we launched *Seedlings*. Then we have added Jimmer Prieto to the "staff," creating wonderful Spanish translations.

The seedlings are getting planted in minds around the world. Cultivated by loving gardeners, they grow, then blossom, then bear spiritual fruit. The harvest of the stories has begun to come in, and it promises to be an abundance of love.

As all spiritually driven souls partner with Father and each other in a cornucopia of rich and varied spiritual pursuits, the bounty of our experience is changing the world. Black Lives Matter, Me Too, people quitting old (sometimes well-paying) jobs, then seeking new ones that satisfy deeper needs. We reap what we sow, prepare a meal for the joyful feast of the harvest.

It's been a very good year.

A Seed

In early childhood, when we make our first moral decision, a seed is planted in our mind. *Wait!* I know what you're thinking... *POD PEOPLE!!!*

This is not a physical seed. My mind is not my physical brain. My mind is part of me, but not a tangible part. For purposes of this piece of writing, however, I'll compare this spiritual seed to a physical seed.

Though planted, this seed has yet to germinate. Inside its shell is the promise of new life. As we grow older, make more and more decisions, germination proceeds. The shell is still solid, but there is new life stirring inside it. A new soul is gestating, in embryonic form.

Sooner or later, we will face adversity. These trials will not be equitable. Some of us will face wealth, some poverty. Some will be nurtured, some neglected or abused. Some will be surrounded by love, some by bigotry and hatred. But it won't be easy for anyone. Period. (Ironically, the best luck is often the worst curse.)

Adversity is good for us! We need it to grow. But growth only occurs when we are truly engaged in life. A newborn chick needs to gain strength through struggling to emerge from its shell. We also need to seek out and struggle with adversity, actively engage in life, find something worth doing that is focused on the betterment of others. The lack of adversity can cause a spiritual drought. A seed can dry up and die if hidden away from the rain.

Each episode of adversity brings a rain cloud. Rain heals the earth. Each rain drop softens the shell of our inner seed. Eventually a crack appears, and a seedling/soul emerges. To grow stronger, it needs to be lovingly nurtured. Our soul sends out leaves and reaches for the Son. The seed begins to sprout, branches out, flowers, one day bears spiritual fruit.

Becomes a Seedling

It's Not You, It's Me

You should have seen this coming; I know *I* did. Things have been changing for some time now. *It's not your fault! You did nothing wrong.* In fact, it was our decisions that got my new partner and I together in the first place. Because of you, I grew. You're the same light-hearted, loving person I remember from the beginning. But our paths and needs have not been the same for years now. I need to move on.

We've been together since childhood. I remember how we used to laugh and play. I'll never forget the pleasure we found in each other's company, and it only increased daily. It felt like everyone wanted to be us. Those memories will last beyond a lifetime.

There were some bad times, of course, as in every relationship. Somehow, we managed to avoid the blame game, took our difficult moments in stride, and triumphed in the end. We were able to pick up the pieces again and again, put the relationship back together.

Inevitably, I began to see your darker side, your bad habits, your selfishness. I don't claim to be a saint; I know that these character faults are all too common in our day and age. You were, if anything, better than most. While I applaud you for that, I found it increasingly inconsistent with my changing life goals. I can't go on living the old life we created. I want a better life.

I've decided to leave you, to move on to a new future with a new partner. In fact, I introduced you two on more than one occasion, but I could tell you were suspicious; those suspicions were well founded as it turned out. What began as a mutual attraction turned into a full-on love affair. I never tried to hide it, and I could tell you were in denial, longed for me to come back to our old life together. But I'm eternally committed to my new partner. Don't worry about the settlement; I've decided to leave everything to you. I'll take nothing with me.

Unlike you, my new partner is completely true, beautiful, and good. But what really attracted me was *the absolute love for me*, which I soon became able to return. The promise of that love is an eternity together, and we will soon be **one**. Yes, we've made the final decision, are promised to each other, this time forever. Death will not do us part.

After an extended honeymoon, we'll begin to learn, work and travel together. You'd be amazed at the connections my new partner has; in places one would never imagine! It's a bit sad that you're bound to stay behind with no future, but it was inevitable.

Adieu, my ego.
I'll never forget our time together.

Can you Ever Forgive Me?

How many mistakes does it take before I stop making the same one? Apparently too many. I've made it time and again. Like making New Year's resolutions, making apologies is easier to do than following through and changing my behavior.

My favorite mistake, at least the one I most often make, is wrongly accusing my wife. Each time I can't find something, my inner reaction is "What have you done with my...?" All too often that accusation pops out before I have a chance to stop it. She always forgives me, but it just makes one more unwanted pinprick in our relationship.

How many times has she forgiven me? It's probably close to seventy times seven. Jesus threw out that number once, meaning that we should never stop forgiving others.

Sometimes trespasses made against us are very difficult to forgive. We hold grudges, let them burrow into our hearts where they fester like sores and corrode our psyches. They damage us far more than the offender ever could have.

Father never holds grudges. He forgives me unconditionally. However, my reception of that forgiveness might be delayed if I have been unable to forgive someone. "As I forgive those who trespass against me" is a real thing. I need to let go of that grudge to make room in my heart for his gift of forgiveness. By giving, I receive.

Sometimes the hardest person to forgive is myself. I've had plenty of occasions to seek forgiveness after the shame of having caused a problem by my thoughtlessness. I forgive myself, but it might take a while to accept forgiveness. Meanwhile, Father has already done so.

Father asks me to be perfect, as he is. He knows that perfection won't happen in a single lifetime. His plan for me is an eternal life with many stops throughout a vast universe. He knows that if I unite with his spirit fragment within me, constantly seeking to do his will, I will gradually become like him.

I wanna grow up to be just like Dad!

Eureka!

California, the Golden State. In 1849, people from around the world became aware of the fabulous riches here for the picking: gold, glistening in stream beds or buried in rich veins, ready to be plucked by dedicated miners. It was the chance of a lifetime for three hundred-thousand hungry, ambitious, hard-working seekers. It even lured some from as far away as China.

Very few ever struck it rich. Many, like Chinese and Native Americans, were exploited in the greed-fest which so often accompanies booms. Impoverished miners were left stranded without money or means of transportation to return to the homes or families abandoned in the excitement.

Needing to find ways to survive in new communities, they did what they already knew how to do, or were willing to struggle and learn. They discovered new means of survival, rebuilt their lives in the land of opportunity. One path out of this world of need lay open to everyone: *service*. Thousands in need of clothing, food, shelter, and jobs drew upon inner strength to provide those things in the service of their fellows.

Our own route to spiritual wealth will be paved with the service of our sisters and brothers. The need is all too plain to see. A new generation of treasure seekers is called upon to uplift our world. The treasure we seek will be spiritual, mining *hearts of gold*. Unlike the miners of old, we'll be lured by the pursuit of true wealth, swap gold fever for spiritual fervor.

Spiritually hungry, ambitious, hard-working people will one day rethink the worldly possessions which weigh us down, augment our poverty. We'll go forth, for some continue, on a quest guaranteed to succeed if faithfully followed. Sincerely seeking this spiritual wealth, we will find the abundant needs spread out before our opened eyes.

Like Jesus before us, we'll find rich treasure in the hearts and minds of the brethren we serve. Like him, we'll inherit vast spiritual wealth, if not in this world, then in the next. Like him, we'll be filled with the joy of sister and brotherhood in Father's family.

You needn't book passage to find this new gold field. It's being revealed right now, before your eyes, right where you live. Untapped wealth resides in that homeless person you just passed by, that stranger in need of a comforting word, that friend weighed down with a heavy burden. You may soon, yourself, joyfully come to the aid of a soul in need, silently say to your Father within,

I have found it!

Who Will Save the Children?

I was born into a temporary family. They were loving parents, and I loved them deeply in return. They provided well for me and my siblings. As I matured, then left the family, I began to lose touch with them. I yearned for what I'd never had – a strong, personal, loving bond with my spiritual mom and dad. I realized much later that they had never forgotten me, had tried repeatedly to connect, understood my struggle, had never wavered in their absolute love for me.

I scoured many locations, actively and passively on their trail for years. I sometimes got clues as to their whereabouts but had yet to fully embrace them. I was near them on more than one occasion. I knew that they were out there, yearning for me to come home to them.

I joined several *Foster-children Anonymous* organizations, meeting others who, like me, had taken up the search for their true parents. Our meetings and activities were solemn, sometimes joyous occasions that I looked forward to at the end of each week. We all were devoted to the quest, exchanged tips and strategies, reinforced all our cherished hopes that our efforts would not be in vain.

Eventually though, some began to abandon the search, filling the void with careers, causes, and families of their own. A few succumbed to despair, finding solace in drugs, sex, or delinquent behavior. My greatest fear, of course, was that one day my own children might feel the same sense of loss. As they grew, then departed, I was faced again with the loneliness of being a lost child.

Then, after years of search I finally found Them, "hiding" in plain sight, in my own heart and soul where they had been all along. I thank *Celestial 23 and Me*, a spiritually based Father/Mother team dedicated to restoring lost children to their deepest roots. I felt the spiritual embrace of my newfound eternal parents for the first time. I've charted a clear path, begun an eternal voyage through the universe, seeking daily to find my way to my final spiritual home.

I owe a huge debt to my earthly parents. From them, I had the faith and courage to trace my spiritual roots. They helped me begin the journey upon which I now proceed.

It's good to be on the way back home again!

Door Number One or Door Number Two?

Have you seen the game show in which a choice must be made about which door opens to the prize and which reveals a "white elephant." Isn't life a little like that? We make decisions every day, not knowing for sure what's in store. Something as simple as deciding when to take a drive can lead to smooth sailing or to a horrible traffic snarl. You never know...

Except...The single most important decision you will *ever* make can be made with *complete certainty* as to its outcome.

Our Father has given us a start in the universe. He has done his best to provide a loving, secure environment in which we can thrive. He knows full well that life will not be *materially* equal, that some of us will be born into plenty and some into poverty. Also, the *ways* of the world are planned by people like you and me, and those plans often don't work out very well, do they.

However, Father does provide *spiritual* abundance for all, equally and absolutely. He is no respecter of persons. He loves each of us without favor. He provides a fragment of his pure spirit of love to dwell inside us, surrounds us with the guidance of Mother's spirit and her angels, and comforts us with the spirit of his son Christ Michael who also dwells within

Whether we welcome or refuse this spiritual wealth is a personal choice. Our free will is absolute. Father, Mother, and Son each refuse to abridge that will, and honor your choices completely. As a parent, you likewise honor your children's wishes. You want what's best for them but cannot, should not, force them to accept even your best-laid plans.

Sooner or later, now or after you leave this world, you will be asked to make a choice. Do you want to open door number one, align your will with that of your Father, or door number two, choose self. He wants the best for you regardless of your choice. Whichever you choose, he will still provide you with spiritual guidance and help in any way he can to make this life rich and rewarding. His love never wavers or favors.

What's behind door number one? Begin a new, spiritual life, an opportunity to expand a relationship with your Universal Father; carry out his life plan for you, feed your soul, seek fusion with your indwelling Father fragment, enjoy an eternal life of spiritual growth, travel the universe, and discover ever more deeply his love for you.

And door number two? You decide that one life as a mortal was good enough for you. You're not interested in more but thank you anyway.

The decision is yours alone.

Drive My Car

It's easy to get obsessed with cars. They serve our needs, sometimes alluring us with promises of status. If we're not careful we can be seduced by their beauty, speed, complete reliability and ever-proliferating new features.

On second thought, they also can have downsides: spewing pollutants, requiring maintenance and cash infusions, and, with some drivers, encouraging recklessness.

I've had the same car as long as I can remember. At the beginning it was cute, even fashionable. Everyone I met adored it. Practically maintenance free and affordable (in fact it was a gift to me); it served me well for many years.

Then the problems began. It often broke down and was involved in some serious accidents. It began to show its age, lost its zippiness and shine and was less and less reliable.

Increasing numbers of people have solved these problems by swapping out for other options. Bicycles are growing in popularity (for thirty years I was an avid cyclist). And sometimes we have no choice but to stop driving, as when I was, for a while, in a wheelchair and a walker.

Time for a trade-in? Maybe a new concept of "car" is in order. How about "life vehicle?"

Long ago, as I saw this transition coming, I began investing in the vehicle of the future. When I take my retirement from earth, I will acquire an upgraded life vehicle, still *me* but designed to house my ever-growing soul. It will get me about in my new surroundings with total comfort and

As I progress through the universe, I will be able to trade it in for a newer, better model repeatedly. When perfected, it will even take me to the center of the universe, to meet my Father who eagerly awaits my arrival. I know he's expecting me. He'll leave the light on.

Happy motoring!

Amazing Technology Breakthrough

Reports are in about a radically different, infallible GPS (Global Positioning System). This system has been proven to be unerring and will never receive a factory recall notice or require updated reprogramming.

This system, little heard of until the last hundred years, seems to have been widely available for some time. Users familiar with it verify claims of its unerring performance, stating it is also extremely user-friendly. Additionally, it never needs repair as proven by the experiences of numerous lifelong users. Even children as young as six can access it, with no previous tech training required.

In fact, this system, SGPS, long ago went global, even universal. Compatible with any life-vehicle on the planet, it is programmed in every language.

Provided freely to everyone on earth, it unerringly guides all on their best individual path to their Father on Paradise. Also known as BFF (Beloved Father Fragment), it will never leave you stranded or helpless.

No more nettlesome voice incessantly telling you what to do ("Turn left in 1/4 mile...Continue on this route...Recalculating...", SGPS, in a still, small voice gently suggests, almost subconsciously, how to proceed on the best path. In fact, experienced travelers will find they can proceed almost on cruise control once they have committed to their destination and consistently yield right of way to their Heavenly Father. (However, both hands on the wheel are always advised when encountering emergency conditions)

(As suggested above, this system has only one built-in destination **Paradise**. It does, however, come with an opt-out clause: any user, even one gaining lifelong benefit from its use, is empowered to cancel the hard-wired destination and simply return their life-vehicle to be recycled when no longer usable.)

Welcome to SGPS!
(Spiritual Galactic Positioning System)

I'm Not From the Best Neighborhood. Does it Show?

Where I came from, life was not really that bad. I mean, there was more crime than most neighborhoods had to put up with, lots of fighting and broken families. Some kids got a decent education, but most of them never made it to college. Still, all things considered, if you really worked at it and got a few good breaks you could do okay for yourself.

Right, good breaks. Here's the thing. if you came from the right "background" you got *all* the good breaks. The fix was in – great jobs, elite schools, extravagant vacations, luxury cars, and mansions (at least compared to *my* house).

Of course, *everyone* had to put up with some pretty ugly stuff. There was greed, selfishness, and unfairness everywhere. It seemed like a lot of people were mainly in it for themselves. Most people just got by, many were desperately poor, while a few were super-rich. But even the "winners" were pretty unhappy. And there wasn't much hope for the future, either.

The worst thing was that so many people gave up hope for a good life. I heard it was even worse back in the old, old days. Then it was a *real* jungle! You had to always watch your back if you didn't belong to the right group. And people could tell by looking at you which group you were in.

A lot of our problems stemmed from a lack of outstanding role models, leaders and teachers who had been around long enough to share a greater vision of how life could be and should be. There was little understanding of why we were even there in the first place. What was the true purpose of life and why did we feel so alone in the universe?

I guess that's different from a lot of the better places most of you came from. I know, everything wasn't perfect in *your* old stomping grounds either, but at least most of you had leaders you could look up to and plenty of shared values. Admit it, at least you had it better than I did.

Yeah, I'm the product of a rough neighborhood, but I'm a survivor. I pulled myself up by my bootstraps. Well, not all by myself. I was one of those who discovered that there were lots of helpers to be found who could introduce you to the right Guide through the maze we called life. It helps to know somebody with connections, but then again, anyone can. You just had to be willing to seek them out and have faith that life could be wonderful if you just gave it a chance. And, ironically, I'm told that all that suffering will actually work out well for me in the end.

**So life looks pretty good here on
Mansonia Number One.
Cool name for a planet!**

What's for Dinner?

Fish tonight? That was the request I got from my wife. I do all the cooking in my family, and I love to cook. Unfortunately, it can also be a real chore. There are many "customers" at any home "café" with unique preferences: Asian, Mexican, organic, vegan... you get the idea. One size does *not* fit all, especially with nutrition. Especially *spiritual* nutrition.

Most religions are built around one size fits all. Each has the right answer to the request for spiritual sustenance –all you need do is pay attention in church, synagogue, or mosque, learn the rules, bring in the right kind of new customers who will follow the "true" path. *There is ONE WAY to get to Heaven, we have the monopoly on access, and we'll share it only with the insiders who think the same as we do.*

However, our Father didn't go to chef school. He doesn't specialize in one cuisine or certain customers. He loves all, especially wants to feed those who aren't hungry yet. He desires a special relationship with each of us, wants us all to be satiated with joyous fellowship. And he knows that there are many individual paths to him. *Individual*, not *institutional*.

Institutional. You know what I mean, McDonalds (where food is quick, cheap, and uniform). Father wants a universe full of powerful individuals aggressively seeking feasts, not automatons settling for a life of culinary ease. Avoiding inconvenience, surviving on easy-to-digest fast food is not a very high goal for a meal *or* for a life.

And that *easy* thing? Pablum is easy-to-digest, but it won't sustain a virile adult. True spirituality is not easily acquired. Religion needs to be something you can sink your teeth into, gnaw to the bone, then crave more.

Father does, however, expect all who seek him to do so with an open, loving heart. He also wants customers to bring their own ingredients, have their own ideas for a personal cuisine, crave heavenly delicacies, learn with and from his highly trained staff (and maybe show *them* something new), create unique, nutritious meals which will entice new customers to venture out of conventional restaurants and do some gastronomically incredible home cooking of their own.

Maybe that home should be open to all starved for a righteous meal, those thirsty for companionship, those who feel locked out of comfortable establishments looking only for their own kind to join them in fellowship.

Does your chef have a credential from Celestial Cuisines?

You Never Forget How to Ride a Bike

I wasn't much older than Jeanette the day I tried to help her learn to ride a bike. Running alongside, holding the bike frame as she pedaled, I kept encouraging her to keep her balance and steer. At one point, I let go of the bike, but continued to run alongside and encourage her. Then I stopped, watched her proceed steadily on her own, and yelled congratulations. "Jeanette, you're riding by yourself!" She suddenly realized she was alone and collapsed into a heap.

A huge part of learning anything is having faith that we *can succeed*. Without faith, failure is inevitable. Encouragement from a friend or a coach can sustain us at first, but once we're alone, fear can creep in. And unreasoned fear is the mortal enemy of faith.

Living our lives without fear is hard. Yet, as infants, we lived fearlessly. We fully trusted our mother and father, took risks daily, somehow survived. Walking, then running, we joyfully explored the world. Somewhere along the way, however, our faith began to erode. Encountering the world, and learning that danger might arise, we began to lock doors and consider self-defense.

Somewhere between extremes exists the right level of trust. I don't fear a knock at my door, but a pounding fist might be a warning. Of course, no one can save us from the inevitable consequence, death. But death is not to be feared. It is the necessary bridge to spiritual reality, not an end but a new beginning.

"Be as wise as serpents, but as harmless as doves," Jesus taught, "Fear not, for I am with you." Alongside us always, especially when we are being tested, he will never abandon us. In our moment of need until our last breath, he is there to spiritually support us, comfort us, join with us as we face life's consequences led by his Spirit of Truth within. Unlike my support withdrawn from Jeanette, Jesus' will never abandon us.

Never forget to trust your faith in our Father/Brother Jesus

The Master Chef's Apprentice

I'm enrolled in a cooking apprenticeship program that I can't recommend highly enough. I am the apprentice to a Master Chef. It is a highly individualized program; I am his only apprentice.

He knows me well, based on proven scientific data. He has accumulated this knowledge from an exhaustive analysis of my unique combination of needs and skills as well as the local ingredients available. He had previous students, all of whom unfortunately couldn't complete the program, but he learned from them how to prepare for working more suitably with me. He has high hopes for our success.

He began this student/client relationship with a series of menus in mind. Not knowing any better back then, I turned down some suggestions that seemed too spicy or contained ingredients with which I wasn't familiar. However, he knew when to adapt to my personal needs. Now I realize I missed out on some spectacular meals.

He includes me in menu planning, too. We have ventured out into the community with some new restaurants, designed to serve my neighbors' needs. We talk frequently about which ingredients are in season and which cuisine to tackle next. He assures me that before he is through, I will become his partner forever. We will open a chain of new restaurants as a team, serving the needs of an ever-expanding clientele.

His goal is not only to improve my cooking output, but also my personal skill set. We work so closely we anticipate incorporating into one Master Chef/apprentice team, Team Us! My daily decisions are essential for this transformation to occur.

I've always wanted to be a good cook. I now aspire to being a master, then a supreme chef. I'm learning from the best how to prepare and serve delicious, nutritious meals to feed the spiritual needs of my fellows. One day we'll travel to some far-away exotic locales, taking on apprentices of our own, together.

Bon Appetit!!

A Call to Arms

There was a man who discovered an impregnable treasure chest, ornately decorated and obviously of great value in and of itself, yet too heavy to carry off and with no obvious means to gain its contents. Wanting access to the treasure inside, he wondered if there was a key hidden away nearby.

Frantically searching the area around him he saw a few rocks but turning them over yielded nothing. The grass around him offered another possible resting place for the key, but combing through it was of no avail. The day was nearing twilight. He finally decided to call for help. Just then he noticed a dull gleam of metal protruding under the corner of the chest, the half-buried key.

Should he open the chest? After all his anguish over it, he doubted he could bear disappointment. But if it was full, how could he bring it safely home if he encountered robbers on the way? He obscured it with branches, then walked away. Knowing where to find it someday when he was ready, he comforted himself with his new awareness.

Jesus told of a man who was given one talent yet lacked faith to use it. He then decided to hoard it lest it be lost. It was taken away from him and given to someone who would act. The challenge that man faced is given to you, given to me. Faith is the key for which we must search. This key, when we dare turn it, compels the acts in which we must engage.

Our world is confronted, as it has been again and again, by hate. Inside that chest which we have been given is a powerful spiritual weapon of love, the power of prayer. This power is greater than the skill of a world leader who wields the weapons of war, of economics, of diplomacy. It is the one gift we have each been given, a gift which gains leverage with every use by every individual. We are called upon to unsheathe this power.

Jesus' legions of angels await the call to action that *we must each of us give.* Our free will is the barrier to that action; unless called upon by our free will choice, spiritual forces cannot involve themselves in our world. Now it is time to sound the call.

A while ago, a group I was in was challenged with finding ways to bring peace. Prayer was brought up, but the unspoken consensus deemed prayer a paper sword with which to confront a tank. Then I recalled a Chinese man who confronted a tank alone, unafraid. I have decided to act, to use my key of faith to unlock and spend the spiritual treasure I have been given. I pray, spiritual brethren, help stop this war. I issue a call for

the arms of the angels.

Another Piece of the Puzzle

A man volunteers in a homeless shelter, a young girl forgives a slight, a mother prays for her child at war. Three more pieces are fit into the puzzle. Every day on this world, there are millions more pieces filled in, for a puzzle the size of the moon. A million years into our evolution, the puzzle-picture would still be only vaguely discernible from earth.

The whole picture, the completed puzzle, is seen only by Father. And he saw it vividly, completely, before the first act of moral choice by the first human on earth, when the first piece of the puzzle was put in place. One day in the far distant future, all will see the glory of the perfected planet we call home. All will treat sisters and brothers with the love so freely given by a spiritual fellowship completely aligned with the will of God. And earth is only one small, inhabited planet in a universe of trillions. These trillions of puzzle-pictures await their solutions.

We celebrate the triumphant life of Jesus, leading a world in chaos into God's loving arms. Yet Father has the same love for him as for each of the millions who daily pray and act in seemingly insignificant ways to make our world slightly more spiritual. Each prayer, by itself nearly invisible, is compounded by countless numbers of small changes in behavior, even if only the behavior of the one who made the prayer.

We little understand the power of prayer and worship. The immensity of the sky above and the task before us on this troubled planet are overwhelming. It's easy to forget that within us is a fragment of the all-powerful creator of the universes, whose will it is that good vanquish evil, love obliterate hate. How much faith do we have that his will actually *be done?*

Why didn't he create a perfect world in the first place? As a parent, put yourself in his place. Don't you want your children to achieve victories and earn their own way? Father wanted us to be co-creators of ourselves and our world. Each of us has a starring role in the part of the puzzle into which we were born. He set out to raise legions of heroes and heroines. The casting call went out long ago, and still reverberates.

There are no small parts, only individual actors.

Mine Is in the Shop

Ever had a loaner car provided by a shop while yours is under repair? It gets you from here to there, it's okay, but it's only meant to be temporary. Once you no longer need it, it's returned. It has served its purpose.

What if your brain is a loaner? You can use it to get around and it's reliable. It might need some work, but it's all you've got. No transplant is available. It's up to you to take care of it the best you can for the rest of your life.

But what if a new one *is* available? No, not in this lifetime. There is a new one now under construction within you. Your body is the shop, and your superconscious is a co-mechanic. Fortunately for you, there is a Master Mechanic, a fragment of God, working alongside your superconscious mind to create a soul.

Each decision you make, good or bad, is fashioned by this team to create the new you, your soul. *Team You. Yay team!!* Piece by piece, under construction from the ground up since you were a child, this new soul-mind is a custom job. It is being designed to serve you personally on your next stop in the universe.

It will need tune-ups, up-grades from world to world. These will be automatic. It's part of the package deal being offered. Offered, not mandated. It is completely your decision whether to accept this new you. If you do so repeatedly you will be gifted with a more powerful model with new features you can't even imagine.

And you thought Maseratis were incredible!

Free Range Critters

We've been adopted by a feral cat. She arrived one day at dinner time, then again for breakfast the next day. She's been with us ever since. Our dog, who only goes out in the back yard, doesn't yet know of her arrival into the family.

We're told not to feed feral cats; they can multiply and might cause problems. But our cat also hunts for rodents: she's earning her keep. She lets us pet her, which is rare. She may be newly homeless.

Most cats who are homeless won't even get close to people. They've mastered the art of survival, eluded capture, when necessary, neither asked for help nor come closer than necessary to the world of humans. Feral cats tend to have short lives, must fight or flee from predators. They often find themselves unwelcome in "polite" society and meet tragic ends.

In contrast to a feral cat, this story you're reading was born into a loving environment, nurtured by a caring author and his spiritual Father who want only the best for it, yearn for it to live on as a virtual free-range story. We know that its time with us is limited to days before it's ready to go feral, leave the litter and join previous feral stories on its world travels.

These feral stories, unlike most religious writing, must "grow legs" to survive on their own. Belonging to no one, they belong to everyone, are free to go where they will and make new friends in the lives and minds of readers I will never meet. They might be shared anew with friends, over and again. Ideally, each will enjoy multiple loving owners during their lifetimes.

But these stories are only glimpses of spirituality. True spiritual growth comes when lives are devoted to true meanings and values, worship of our heavenly Father who dwells within and the loving service of his other children. These feral stories and their offspring are only one more path forward on that journey. One day, though, I hope to see them again, reflected in a life they have helped to change.

Who knows, they may have as many as nine lives!

The Little Things

Father loves the little things we do. They show our true character. Our lifetime and its million small acts of love are part of a handwoven tapestry of grand design in his eyes. One tiny thread, broken, can rend the garment. That thread repaired can save it. These small acts define us for who we really are; they demonstrate our unquestioning, reflexive acts of faith and reliably loving decisions in times of small crises. They mean more to him with his panoramic vision than do the mighty moments of those earthly heroes who finally came through when needed in the end. The smiles of children are of more consequence than the thunder of champions.

Nothing done in love is trivial. Nothing done in hate is real. Evil acts are forgotten in time as though they never were, are mere shadows behind love's stunning beauty. Love's colors are best seen when in contrast to the darkness surrounding them. That darkness, that background, is invisible; the eye is drawn to the beauty to which darkness gives only definition, outline and clarification. It is love's beauty which commands our deepest devotion.

Our own universe journeys began long ago when we were children, probably through some small act of kindness; maybe a decision to let someone else benefit at our expense, or perhaps lending a hand for a friend in need. Every individual kindness is remembered by our Father. In fact, the most important small acts are often so effortless, so seamless that they escape our own awareness. We see our movie frame by frame; he sees the whole picture, from beginning to end, as a unified body of work.

He gives greater weight to those many moments of love than to lapses of judgment which disrupt lives and carry weighty penalties. Small, loving acts slowly erode unreal mistakes, repair our soul, redefine our reality.

Jesus loved his time with small children. He would sometimes suspend the most profound moments of his life and allow them to become the center of attention. They were his purpose, his meaning, the symbols of his message of Father's love and a demonstration of how we all should respond to one another, with simplicity, purity, kindness, graciousness, and love. May we all learn well from the children, who have not yet forgotten what life is about.

The true path is created one footstep at a time.

She Saw Something in Me

The day we eloped she saw something in me, though I couldn't see it myself. I was an unemployed college dropout stoner at the time. My worldly possessions included an electric guitar and a few hundred dollars from the insurance company for the car I had just wrecked (for which I lost my driver's license). Oh yeah, and I was about to be shipped off to Vietnam. But she had faith that I would be a good father and husband.

Fifty-four years later, I'm glad she had faith in me; faith, the ability to see and believe in things that are not at all apparent and have yet to be proven in any way. Father also had faith in me at that low point, even though I had lost faith in him. I had just recently concluded that my church upbringing needed new depth. I slowly began rebuilding a spiritual life, casting broader and deeper than before.

Father has faith in all of us, even in those showing the least promise to people around them. He knows us better than we know ourselves, knows that all are potentially new members of his loving family. Where we see a lost cause or a political nightmare, he sees a new child with unlimited future spiritual promise. He never gives up on anyone.

We live in a deeply divided world with sharp edges and little room for compromise. We have grown callous toward those who think, act, and believe differently than we do. We seek out those who share our perspectives and values and show disdain for those whose beliefs and choices clash with ours. We open our bubble to only the right people.

I have so much to learn about seeing something in everyone just as he does. I have yet to remember to look into the eyes of everyone knowing that our Father is within them, loves them as deeply as he loves me despite the differences which seem to distance us.

I'm continually humbled by the faith Father has in me. Again and again, I fall far short of my goal for perfection of purpose, let alone of achievement. I need to be accepting of my own shortcomings before I can truly be accepting of others'. I thank Jesus and the angels for their continuous efforts on my behalf. With them on my side I can't fail, because...

Father sees something in me.

The Soul Crafters

No, I don't mean a cobbler; that's for a *sole*. And when was the last time you went to a cobbler for shoes, a tailor for clothes, even a farmer for fresh eggs? Our world is fast, cheap, discardable, mass market and ASAP! Most things are made to be quickly replaced by a newer model.

When you *do* need an expert, just ask around. If it's a real pro you want, his/her reputation is usually well established. But the best of the best? They're rare indeed, usually out of our price range, and the wait time can be prohibitive.

But if your *inner* soul needs repair, I have just the team for you! They've been around forever. They were the ones who began your soul's creation (with your unwitting help; you've been responsible for making key decisions along the way since you were young.)

It's a Mom/Pop/Son family outfit. The Son's in charge of the local franchise, but they work as a team, always available. They make house calls, provide service around the clock, and have an amazing staff! They will design and carry out the perfect personal plan for your soul's birth, upkeep, and growth.

It all begins with a thorough analysis of your soul's needs. In fact, your personal information is already in their data base. Careful listeners, they can readily tell if your self-description is accurate, though they're very discreet and allow ample time for you to realize your genuine needs more fully.

The next step involves community service; this is always put toward credit for payment. (We'll get into cost later.) It's a pay-as-you-go type of thing, and you'll be given regular assignments which can more than amply cover the cost of soul growth.

This soul building service fits in nicely with your personal skill set, so you're always able to complete assignments when you try hard enough. If new skills are required, they can be taught by their expert staff or at a local educational institution. And the jobs they find for you? Mine are great!

They're pricey, but the daily installment plan is affordable, just prayer, worship, communion, and service. (You'll be making those payments for an eternity.) The burden is light, and the yoke is easy. They'll be with you every step of the way, will never leave, even when the work is complete. And happily, it never will be. Tell a friend! New souls are always in high demand.

Angels are standing by 24/7. Use your My-phone.

1(800) Souls-R-Us

From a Lowly Caterpillar...

It is estimated that within seven to ten years every cell in the human body will have been replaced. That means I have been rebuilt between seven and ten times in my lifetime. That's just the physical part, but let's look at that as an analogy.

We are immersed in Mother's holy spirit, and in-dwelt by Jesus' Spirit of Truth and Father's pure spirit fragment, simultaneously joining us around age six (110:6.13). During my lifetime I have repeatedly asked them to transform me. I know that when I worship Father, that act alone causes me to become more like him.

My spiritual self goes through the same process as my body. My soul is growing decision by decision. The trajectory of that spiritual evolution moves forward each time I pray, worship or act in sync with Father's will, affirm my commitment to live to the best of my ability in accordance with my best understanding of that divine will.

We don't all begin at the same spiritual place, nor do we all progress forward at the same rate. But the goal will assuredly be attained by all. The path, velocity, and trajectory are uniquely personal but uniformly inevitable. We pursue this path knowing we will grow from the mortal into the spiritual children of God.

This transformation is happening right now, relentlessly replacing my mortal mind with its soul counterpart. My soul is daily building my mind in God's image as I become soul identified.

Now we come to the hardest part of this transformation: *why is it taking so long?* Impatience is a part of our natural inheritance. It has guided us forward since the beginning of human evolution. It prompted us to get things done. We needed it. But we now need to outgrow it.

Father isn't done with me yet. He's in no hurry to do so. He needs me to be constantly confronted with my limitations and to grow beyond them, to work as a partner with him as I deal with life's problems.

I am one of the lucky mortals from a planet lacking visible spiritual support. I am destined to have more severe growing pains than most as I live a life which demands deeper faith. He wants me to have no easy time of it, to be thoroughly time-tested, face countless trials, make thousands of decisions, trust his sure yet often faintly discernible guidance. But then, one day,

a brand new me will emerge.

Stop the Presses!

This just came across the news desk... Our crack team of Pulitzer Prize winning investigative journalists have, through painstaking, relentless work, broken this story wide open, uncovered the news of the century! We've discovered that financial/social injustice and disparity are a serious worldwide scandal. Nowhere on earth is there a single nation, even a large subsection of any population, honestly dedicated to equal distribution of either wealth or justice. Stay tuned for the latest in this ongoing story...

I don't think so.

One day, history students will be astonished to learn that in our current era widespread hoarding of wealth and power was not only tolerated but envied and celebrated. That many of the heroes, icons, and idols of today, the billionaires, superstars, sports champions, politicians, even clerics, were greedy, selfish, corrupt at heart, and in it for their own interests. Even worse, endemic racism, sexism, disease, pollution, global degradation, crime, drugs, and exploitation were pervasive problems that were ignored, denied, or met with a mere shrug of the shoulders. "It's just the way things are."

There are now and always have been some thriving niches in which abundant true wealth is widely and freely available to any and all regardless of financial or social status. Personal growth and happiness are high priorities here, service rather than profit is the social motive, racial diversity and equality are prized social assets, children are loved and esteemed. In fact, love is the widespread social goal toward which its denizens are dedicated.

You need no passport to move into this state, and all are welcomed as legal citizens. Immigration is encouraged and rewarded. Ironically, we were all born there, but most of us were gradually pried away early on and drawn into the shadowy reality to which we have now grown accustomed.

This ideal homeland is known as the family of God, a state of mind and of spiritual grace. It is a reality to which all are implored to relocate. Our loving Father, Mother, and Son are in charge here, filling and surrounding every individual with the truth, beauty and goodness which are characteristic of the loving universe barely visible on, but pervasive beyond earth. There is one prerequisite to citizenship in this state. You must love and worship our Universal Father, himself the perfect embodiment of love, and forsake the false idols so highly valued by popular culture. For some, that will be too steep a price to pay; they prefer things just the way they are.

Read all about it, in the big blue book.

Sending Out an S.O.S.

We all know what to do if we were to be stranded on an island in the middle of the ocean... put a message in a bottle and throw it out to sea. Then begin to pray. The action comes first, because we need to do all we can do before we ask for help.

Monica and I have been engaged in a service which turns this strategy on its head. In the old scenario, the one who needs help throws out the message. We, on the other hand, throw out a helpful message, hoping it might wash up on some distant shore in time to help a person who can benefit from it.

Help comes in many forms, maybe even to someone who never would have thought to seek it. It can be as simple as provoking a welcome smile. Tell me you've never needed that. Other times, it comes just as a friend's dilemma is on your mind, reinforces your idea for how to assist.

Occasionally, we receive an email from a *Seedlings* reader telling us how a story has arrived in a timely fashion in their life, *coinciding* with a larger issue they were dealing with. We humans are in a key position to be material conduits for spiritual assistance.

Coinciding? There are no coincidences. God works in mysterious ways, creates, or takes advantage of anything that might assist one of his children. Countless celestial hosts hover around us, sometimes planting seeds in our minds that will one day be fruitful in a life, sometimes harvesting that fruit to share with someone else never once even encountered by the farmer. The act is ours, the consequences God's. And small acts can have huge impacts.

To be of service. That is the engine of a spirit driven life. What Monica and I offer is just another service. If it's useful... wonderful. If it's not, nothing has been lost; and who knows what the future may hold? You're free to use it one day or not, as needed.

But we implore you to join in this service. Please broadly spread any story that touches you; there may be someone, somewhere who will find it through a friend, on a bulletin board, in a church flyer or in the local paper. It might just fill a need in someone's life. And of course, once these stories leave the garden, they are feral, owned by no one, free to be translated, transformed, restated, quoted from... use your imagination. I know we do.

Spiritual Opportunities Surround us.

About the Author

In my twenties, *The Urantia Book* led me to a career of teaching young children. Jesus taught that we should trust in our Universal Father's love, just as they do. My life's goal is to be as a young child. God is love. Only love can turn this world around.

Printed in the USA
CPSIA information can be obtained
at www.ICGtesting.com
CBHW031332110524
8113CB00002B/8